ALTRINCHAM
THROUGH TIME
Steven Dickens

AMBERLEY

About the Author

Steven is from the Flixton area of Trafford and is married to Sarah – they have three sons and three daughters. He is a retired charge nurse and college lecturer, with an academic background in modern history. He has always had an interest in local history and genealogy and has written several journal and magazine articles on these subjects in the past, as well as writing several Through Time titles.

This book is dedicated to the memory of Barbara Dickens.
Thanks for everything, mum.

First published 2016

Amberley Publishing
The Hill, Stroud, Gloucestershire, GL5 4EP
www.amberley-books.com

Copyright © Steven Dickens, 2016

The right of Steven Dickens to be identified as the Author of this work has been asserted in accordance with the Copyrights, Designs and Patents Act 1988.

ISBN 978 1 4456 3901 7 (print)
ISBN 978 1 4456 3913 0 (ebook)

All rights reserved. No part of this book may be reprinted or reproduced or utilised in any form or by any electronic, mechanical or other means, now known or hereafter invented, including photocopying and recording, or in any information storage or retrieval system, without the permission in writing from the Publishers.

British Library Cataloguing in Publication Data.
A catalogue record for this book is available from the British Library.

Origination by Amberley Publishing.
Printed in Great Britain.

Appointed GPSR EU Representative: Easy Access System Europe Oü, 16879218
Address: Mustamäe tee 50, 10621, Tallinn, Estonia
Contact details: gpsr.requests@easproject.com, +358 40 500 3575

Introduction

The earliest evidence of prehistoric human occupation in the Altrincham area comes from the discovery of two Neolithic arrowheads, and further artefacts found at Dunham. There are also remains in the Broadheath area of the Roman road that ran from Chester (Deva Victrix) to York (Eboracum). The name Altrincham first appears as 'Aldringeham,' or 'homestead of Aldhere's people.' Until the Norman Conquest, Altrincham's manors were owned by the Saxon thegn Alweard. After this they were owned by Hamon de Massey, with the earliest reference to Altrincham being from 1290, when it was granted a charter as a free borough by Baron Hamon de Massey V. It had a weekly market and was possibly a planned market town, established in order to gain income through taxes on trade. The borough was ruled by a court leet and has elected a mayor since at least 1452. This system kept the peace and regulated markets and fairs until its abolition in 1886. Altrincham Fair became St James' Fair, or Sanjam, in 1319 and continued until 1895.

The town is also the location of Dunham Massey Hall. It was the home of the Earls of Stamford, until the 10th Earl's death in 1976; it is now a tourist attraction, owned by the National Trust. There are three Grade I-listed buildings within its grounds and a deer park, which dates back to medieval times. The woodland park contains many ancient oaks, dating back to the seventeenth century and it is a Site of Special Scientific Interest, due to its biodiversity. It remains both an economic and social asset to the area.

Altrincham is an affluent commuter town, which had a population of 45,809 in 2011. Its excellent transport links remain a prime reason for its continuing popularity. In 1754, a stretch of road to the south of Altrincham on the Manchester–Chester route was 'turnpiked'. In 1765 the Timperley–Sale stretch of road suffered the same fate, followed by Altrincham–Stockport in 1821. The improved transport links resulted in market gardening developing in the area. This was aided by the construction of warehouses at Broadheath, along the banks of the Bridgewater Canal, by 1767. A decade later, by 1776, the canal was connected to the River Mersey, giving direct access to the growing market of Manchester, the Irish Sea and other national and international markets.

In 1849 it was the turn of the Manchester South Junction and Altrincham Railway (MSJ&AR) to stimulate both the economic and social development of Altrincham. The town saw a massive increase in its population and developed as an affluent suburb of Manchester, which it remains today. In the twentieth century the growth of motor transport meant that Altrincham's position on the A56 Manchester–Chester main route was of prime importance once motorways were constructed through the area – the M6, M56 and M60. Later, the improvement of the public transport infrastructure, with the introduction of Metrolink trams, helped to maintain Altrincham's reputation as a popular place to live.

Stamford Park was established in order to cater for the recreational needs of Altrincham's rapidly growing population. It was designed by landscape gardener John Shaw and opened in 1880, with cricket and football pitches established for local sporting needs. The land was donated by the 7th Earl of Stamford, George Grey. The park is Grade II listed. There is also Denzell Gardens and the Devisdale in Bowden, which passed to the local authority and public use in 1936. In Broadheath, Altrincham had a distinct and separate industrial area. Founded in 1885 by the 8th Earl of Stamford, Harry Grey, its purpose was to attract business to an already prosperous market town. By 1900 Broadheath had its own docks, warehouses and electricity generating station. Companies, like the Linotype and Machinery Company, employed thousands of workers and created 172 workers' houses near its factory. The Broadheath industrial area has now been regenerated as a retail park. In 1937 Altrincham was granted a charter of incorporation and became a municipal borough. It became a part of the Metropolitan Borough of Trafford on 1 April 1974. Conservation areas, in the Borough consist of The Down, The Devisdale, Bowden, Ashley Heath, Goose Green, Old Market Place, Sandiway, George Street, Linotype Housing Estate, Stanford New Road, Dunham Woodhouses, Dunham Town, South Hale and Hale Station.

There are a number of notable people who have lived in Altincham: the artist Helen Allingham, born in 1848, lived in Altrincham and Bowdon during her childhood; Alison Uttley wrote the Little Grey Rabbit books while living in Bowdon; dramatist Ronald Gow lived in Altrincham during his youth, later teaching at the local grammar school; Hewlett Johnson, known as the 'Red Dean' of Canterbury, was curate and then vicar of St Margaret's parish church from 1904–24. The late Christopher Sievey (Frank Sidebottom), musician and comedian, and Caroline Aherne, comedian, writer and actress, were both residents of Timperley.

This book traces the changes that have taken place in the district over the last 150 years and includes the town centre of Altrincham and its surrounding districts of Bowdon, Dunham Massey, Hale, Hale Barns and Timperley. It charts the district's development from an agricultural economy to an industrial and suburban location, along with the transport developments that influenced this growth. Altrincham's recreational pastimes such as the Garrick Playhouse, Altrincham Football Club, the Hippodrome and its parks and historical buildings are noted, as are its numerous places of worship and the rich history surrounding them.

For technical help relating to some of the photographs in this volume I am indebted to my daughter, Nadia Dickens. I hope that *Altrincham Through Time* will provide the reader with an insight into the way this ancient market town has changed and developed over 700 years to become the modern and popular commuter suburb that we have today.

Old Market Place, Altrincham, 1962
The Orange Tree Inn building dates from 1679 and is reputedly haunted. The restored stocks, where floggings were administered until the early nineteenth century, are also here. The market cross remains and is close to the Old Market Tavern (formerly the Unicorn) and the town hall. The Old Market Place is thought to stand on the site of the original Saxon settlement and is now a conservation area; the cobblestone paving dates from 1896. The Buttermarket stood here from the seventeenth to the late nineteenth century.

Red Lion Hotel, Old Market Place, Altrincham, c. 1900

The Red Lion Hotel (on the left above) and the Unicorn Hotel were built on what was originally a Saxon settlement. The hotels became a stopping point for coaches between Manchester and Chester. Some of these coaches can be seen in the original photograph from around 1900. The Red Lion was used as a billet by the troops of 'Bonnie Prince Charlie' when they came to Altrincham in 1745. The Unicorn Hotel was adjacent to Altrincham's first town hall, built by Lord Delamer in 1849.

The Old Bank, Old Market Place, Altrincham, 1912
The former Lloyds bank was built by George Truefitt for a local banker, William Cunliffe Brooks, in 1877 and continues as commercial premises into the twenty-first century. The whole of this side of Old Market Place was occupied by houses. This includes a public house, the Waggon & Horses, which was demolished to make way for the construction of the bank and the opening of the turnpike route, known as Dunham Road. Carriages used to line along here, awaiting business.

THE NEWEST ARRIVALS at Byroms Mens Shop.

Ready to Wear Hand Woven Harris Tweed Sports-Coats.

Simpson Tailored Riding Macs.

Union and Cotton Gaberdine Raincoats.

Fine Grade Lambs Wool lined Tan Cape Gloves.

Good quality Winter Weight Pyjamas.

Medium weight Underwear by Jaeger.

Customers say :—

It's a pleasure to Shop where everyone is so polite and helpful. That's what I like about "Byroms." You too, will be a welcome visitor at

BYROMS
6, 8 & 10 KINGSWAY, ALTRINCHAM
Established 1851.
Phone ALTRINCHAM 3231 (3 lines).

Byroms Men's Shop, Kingsway, Altrincham, 1946
This was one of the oldest family businesses in Altrincham, being established by James Byrom who was mayor in 1880. The original shop once stood on part of the site later occupied by Lloyds Bank in Old Market Place, then moved across the road and lower down Kingsway. In 1886 J. W. Byrom, mayor in 1901, succeeded to the business. He was followed by his son, Jack Byrom, who was influential in the Altrincham Garrick Society. It was the first Altrincham store to display electric lights; the shop closed in 1970.

Unicorn Hotel, Old Market Place, Altrincham, 1904
In 1814 Thomas de Quincey (1785–1859) wrote about the Old Market Place in *Confessions of an English Opium Eater* while travelling from Manchester to Chester, describing it thus,

> Fruits, such as can be had in July, and flowers were scattered about in profusion: even the stalls of the butchers, from their brilliant cleanliness, appeared attractive: and bonny young women of Altrincham were all tripping about in caps and aprons coquettishly disposed.

Altrincham had changed little since his last visit, fourteen years earlier.

ALTRINCHAM OLD MARKET PLACE,
ABOUT THE YEAR 1826,
SHOWING MARKET HALL, DUNGEON, UNICORN HOTEL,
AND ROUNDABOUT HOUSE.

Old Market Place, Altrincham, *c.* 1826

This interesting print of an original engraving shows the market hall, dungeon, Unicorn Hotel and Roundabout House, in the centre of the Old Market Place. The Buttermarket stood here from the seventeenth century until the late nineteenth century. The Unicorn Hotel was adjacent to the old town hall from 1849, until it was rebuilt around 1900. Local justice was administered from the Unicorn Hotel, hence the presence of the dungeon and stocks in the Old Market Place.

Court Leet, Altrincham, Wednesday 30 October 1901

The court leet saw the election of court officers at the Michaelmas Assize (September–December), for the Barony of Dunham Massey, before the burgesses and aldermen. Court officers dealt with issues that brought defaulters before the courts. They were to legislate regarding the collection of rents and other services due to the lord of the manor. In ancient times tenants were required to grind their corn in the lord's mill. Rubbish collection and building repairs were also part of the court's remit. The buildings is now the Old Market Tavern.

Altrincham Court Leet.

John Wm. Byrom,
Mayor.

Town Hall, Altrincham.

Wednesday, 30th October, 1901.

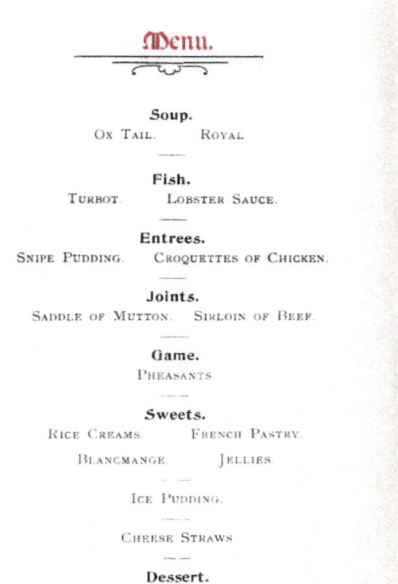

Court Leet, Altrincham, menu and toasts, Wednesday 30 October 1901

Included in the toasts were those concerning the burgesses, constables and the officers of court leet. It was the responsibility of the court leet to ensure that constables, bailiffs, overseers of the poor, surveyors of the highways and other court appointed officers were doing their duty. Another toast was to the town and trade of Altrincham. Trade was protected by the court leet, which ensured that weights, measures and prices were regulated and that produce was of the required standard.

Altrincham Unitarian Chapel, Dunham Road, c. 1910
The chapel was built in 1872, replacing an earlier chapel of 1814 in the town. Its architect was Thomas Worthington, some of whose relatives were long-term members of the chapel's congregation. The three stained-glass memorial windows at the front of the chapel were a later addition. The original windows, displaying flowers, plants and the seasons, are on the south side of the chapel. The chapel, located on the busy Dunham Road, is close to the Old Market Place.

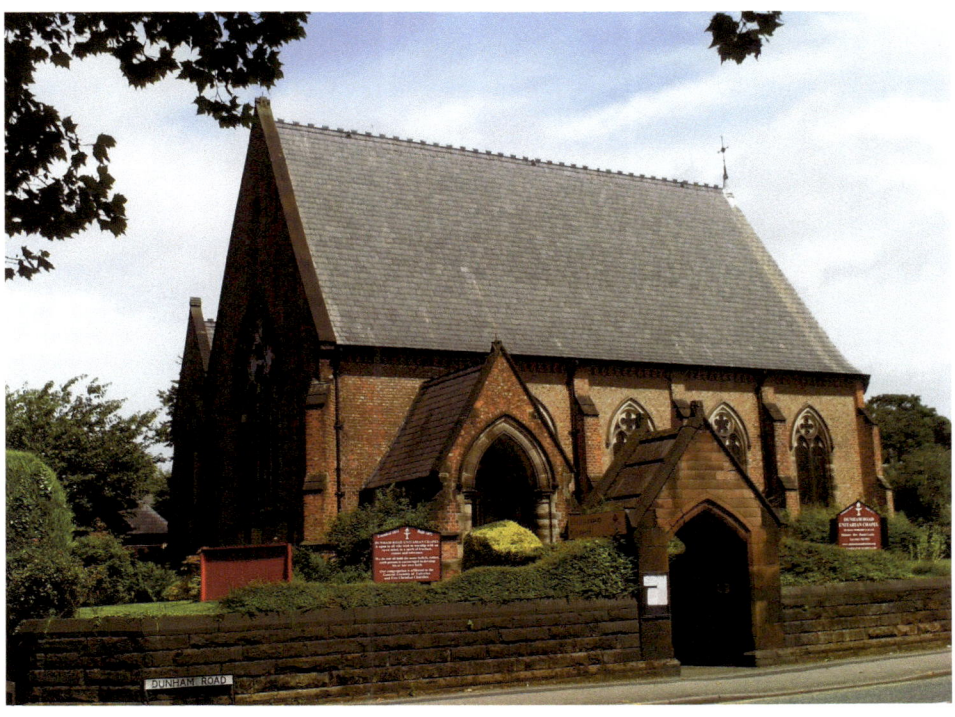

Altrincham Town Hall, Market Street, 1917
The first town hall was established in 1849, adjacent to the Unicorn Hotel. This was replaced by the town hall, shown above, which was built in 1900 (extended 1930). It was home to the Altrincham Urban District Council, which was formed in 1894. In 1974 Altrincham became a part of Trafford Metropolitan Borough Council and in 2004 Altrincham town hall was refurbished, creating a community facility and venue for meetings. The Victorian exterior of the building has been retained, as shown below.

The Market Place, Market Street, Altrincham, c. 1905
In 1290 Altrincham was granted a royal charter by Edward I, enabling the establishment of a market. This was followed by the creation of a borough charter by the de Massey family. The charter allowed a weekly market to be held on Tuesdays (now also Fridays and Saturdays). In 1880 the present market hall was erected at a cost of just over £5,000, and in 1930 the whole of the adjacent land was covered with a glass roof and iron pillars.

Altrincham Hospital, junction of Regent Road and Market Street, c. 1900

As the nineteenth century progressed, Altrincham developed from a market town into a commuter suburb of industrial Manchester. It became an area of great contrasts: from the mansions of Manchester's cotton merchants to the working-class housing situated at the lower end of Altrincham. A Board of Health Report on the housing conditions of the poor led to the construction of a new hospital (which has since been replaced) along Market Street, on land donated by the 7th Earl of Stamford.

George Street, Altrincham, c. 1895
One of the principal shopping streets of the town, the Methodist New Connexion chapel and the Salvation Army hall were also located here. The Methodist church began in Norman's Place, where a church and school opened in 1821 and a larger school in 1860. The church closed in 1966. Some of the businesses seen include: Mason's at No. 85, a hosiers and hatters; George Roberts & Sons at No. 89, a butchers; and John Ingham at No. 93, a China dealer.

George Street, Altrincham, c. 1950
George Street was designated a conservation area on 12 March 1987 and is currently considered 'at risk,' as a result of changing shopping trends. Historically, George Street was the centre of the medieval Lower Town, where artisans, workers' houses and workshops were located. The boundaries of some existing properties trace medieval burgage plots. These properties have varying styles of construction, including Georgian, Victorian and twentieth-century design. George Street was essentially a residential area in the Victorian period but is now a commercial district.

George Street, Altrincham, c. 1960
The number of Victorian commercial properties on George Street shows us the rapid development of Altrincham in this period. The ground floors of most of the Victorian properties along George Street have been developed as retail or commercial outlets. Architectural detail is retained on the first and second floors, where the historic character of these buildings is displayed. Building materials from the local area have been used in their construction, creating a uniform and harmonious appearance.

Old Houses, Lower George Street, Altrincham, 1905
Lower George Street was originally known as Well Street, with the sixteenth-century thatched cottages (shown above), opposite the old library and the police lockups, which date from 1838. A well, known as 'Big Well', was located at Well Lane, later known as Victoria Street (*inset*). One of the cottages was occupied by William Ashley, an Overseer of the Parish. All these structures were demolished in the late 1970s when Petros Developments built the modern shopping centre.

Railway Street, looking towards Altrincham Railway Station, 1907
The first tram through Altrincham made its inaugural journey from the foot of the Downs in 1907. The lines upon which it ran were leased by the district council to Manchester Corporation Tramways for twenty-three years. When this lease expired, omnibus services had established themselves to such an extent that the tram services were withdrawn altogether – the last tram departed for Altrincham on 6 June 1931. Behind the shops on the right, built in around 1895, lay the original Altrincham and Bowdon railway station.

Railway Street, looking towards Bowdon, 1907
Opened on 22 September 1849, the Bowdon terminus of the Manchester, South Junction and Altrincham Railway (behind the shops on the left), became car sheds after the closing of the facility in 1881. Later, in 1931, the depot was made ready for the electrification of the Altrincham to Manchester route. The site closed in December 1991, becoming a car park, as Metrolink did not require it for their services. In 1907 it was used as an engine shed and surrounded by retail premises. It is currently the site of Altrincham Hospital.

Railway Street Tram Terminus, Altrincham, c. 1920

The building forming a junction with Regent Road, on the left, is the Stamford Hotel, which has since been demolished and replaced by a tower block. The building behind the tram, with a triangular turret, was a branch of Martin's Bank, later a Barclays Bank. The single-storey shops on the right have all been demolished and replaced by a 'mixed use retail development', linking in to the Goose Green area behind. Altrincham Hospital is now located on Railway Street, opposite Regent Road.

Railway Street Tram Terminus, Altrincham, c. 1909
The picture above is one of the new, closed-top trams. Trams to Deansgate were later given the number '48', a trend continued by the omnibus services for many years. It was possible to travel by tram from the Downs to Park Road, Timperley for 1d. Tram passengers would have seen many small family retailers along Railway Street, including John Hewson Needham, butcher; Benjamin Battman, florist; and Frederick Johnson, jewellers and watchmaker (the premises later becoming Lepps Jewellers).

Stamford New Road, at its junction with Regent Road, Altrincham, c. 1907

The Stamford name is found on a number of buildings and roads throughout the town today, such as Stamford New Road. The earliest known residence in Altrincham was the Knoll on Stamford Street, near the centre of the medieval town. The Earl of Stamford's seat at Dunham Massey Hall came to the Grey family in 1758. The Stamford family remained influential in the town until the late twentieth century after the death of Roger Grey, the 10th Earl of Stamford, in 1976.

Stamford New Road, Altrincham, c. 1915

Stamford New Road was constructed around 1880, giving Railway Street direct access to the railway station. Several cottages, the old Orange Tree public house and the thatched Faulkners Arms were demolished. Two modern hotels were built in their place, on both sides of the new road. The Faulkners Arms, opposite the Stamford Hotel, retained its name. The land here originally consisted of orchards and vegetable gardens, which bordered both sides of the road as late as 1890, until office and retail developments spread.

Stamford New Road, looking towards Altrincham Railway Station, c. 1950

Altrincham Post Office can be seen on the left above, where there is a gas lamp on the pavement outside the entrance. It was built by J. H. Brown – including the adjoining block of shops – from the designs of John Macnamara, a well-known local architect. In 1905 Charles Heathcote & Sons built Station Buildings (seen on the far right of the inset) for J. H. Brown, adjoining Altrincham Station and now Stamford House. Grade II listed, together with the Station Hotel (below) opposite and the clock tower, they mark the northern boundary of the conservation area.

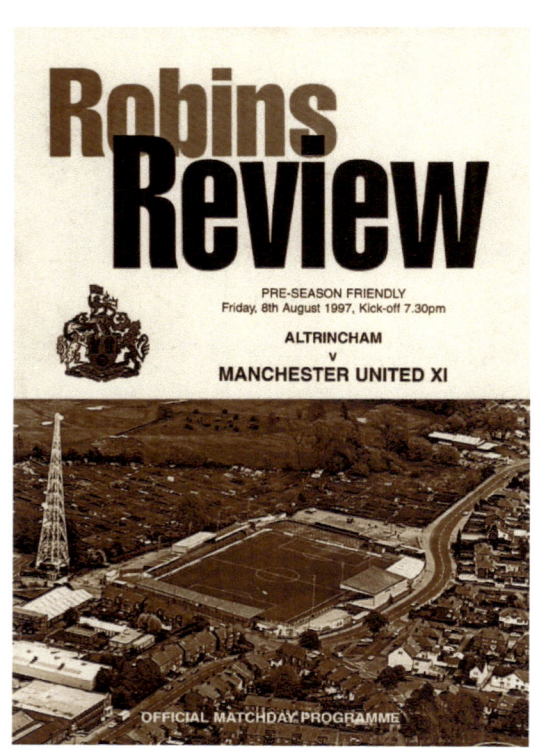

Altrincham Football Club, Moss Lane, Altrincham, 1997

Founded around 1891, Altrincham's stadium has a 6,085 capacity. They currently play in the National League North. For most of their early history they played in the Cheshire County League and became relatively successful in the 1960s and '70s, almost attaining league status. They have a reputation for being FA Cup 'giant killers', holding the record of knocking out more league sides than any other team that has spent its playing history in non-league football. They are previous winners of the FA Trophy.

Altrincham Interchange, Stamford New Road, 2013 and 2016

When the Manchester, South Junction and Altrincham Railway opened to electric trains in 1931, it served a rapidly growing residential district between the two destinations. The line was approximately 8.75 miles in length. Upon opening it had a total single-track mileage, including sidings, of 28 miles. The line was originally quadrupled between the Old Trafford and Sale stations. The railway linked into the national network, including nearby Chester. Recent improvements left the old clock tower standing as a Grade-II listed structure.

Altrincham Railway Station Approach and the Earl of Stamford's 'Homecoming', 1906
The Earl and Countess of Stamford are shown proceeding along Stamford New Road and Station Approach. They are with their son Roger and his sister Lady Jane Grey on their return to take up residence at Dunham Hall in June 1906. Roger became the 10th (and last) Earl and Lord of the Manors of Altrincham, Dunham, Bowdon, Carrington and Bollington, in a lineage stretching back to before 1460. He died on 18 August 1976, aged seventy-nine, his funeral being at St Mark's, Dunham Massey (see inset) on 26 August 1976.

Altrincham Railway Station, Stamford New Road, 1881
The first railway station served Altrincham from 1849–81, and was constructed by the Manchester, South Junction & Altrincham Railway. It opened on 20 July 1849 and was originally located just south of Stockport Road level crossing, near its junction with Stamford Street. It remained here until 4 April 1881, when Altrincham and Bowdon station opened. Bowdon station to the south, at the junction of Railway Street and Lloyd Street, closed at the same time. There are no surviving remains of the Stockport Road Station site.

Altrincham Railway Station and Clock Tower, Stamford New Road, *c.* 1910

Altrincham's North signal box opened in April 1908 and was decommissioned on 7 July 1991; South signal box was decommissioned on 14 July 1968. The station changed its name to Altrincham on 6 May 1974. In 1975 a new booking office was opened on Platform 4 and work to convert the forecourt on Stamford New Road into a bus station began. The canopy over the entrance was removed. It reopened in November 1976 as Altrincham Interchange. Later, on 15 June 1992, Metrolink opened. The Interchange was completely redeveloped and officially reopened on 7 December 2014.

Altrincham Railway Station, Stamford New Road, c. 1900
Altrincham goods yard closed on 8 October 1966 and the level crossing closed on 30 October 1978, being replaced by a bridge carrying the A560. Manchester to Altrincham electric trains ceased on 24 December 1991, with Platforms 1 and 2 later reopening for Metrolink trams. A new roof for Platform 1 was constructed in 2006. Altrincham Interchange has four platforms in total, with two through platforms for services between Manchester Piccadilly and Chester, via Stockport.

Altrincham North Signal Box, *c.* 1931 and Stockport Road Bridge, 2016

The signal box controlled the junction and level crossing at the north end of Altrincham station. The delays to road traffic on Stockport Road (up to twelve trains per hour passed this point) led to the level crossing being replaced by the road bridge in the 1970s. Soon after the signal box was decommissioned in 1991; it was demolished to allow for the introduction of the Metrolink system.

Pioneer System Electric Train, MSJ&AR, 1931, and Stamford House, 2016

It ran from Manchester London Road Station, across a viaduct for 1.75 miles to Cornbrook, where it connected to the Cheshire Lines Committee railway. From Cornbrook it ran through a cutting to a short tunnel immediately before Old Trafford Station. From there it ran through flat country to Altrincham, then continued to Chester, via Knutsford. The grand Stamford House, by Altrincham station, has recently been renovated for use as offices and retail.

Pioneer System Electric Train Souvenir Brochure, 1931 and Altrincham Interchange, looking towards Chester, 2016

The brochure boasted: 'The whole of the electrical equipment at Old Trafford and Timperley substations for the Manchester–Altrincham electrification has been supplied and installed by the British Thomson-Houston Co. Ltd. The equipment includes EHT Switchgear ... and a 1,500 KW Mercury Arc Rectifier – the first 1,500-volt rectifier for British railway electrification ... The complete electrical equipment of the coaches was manufactured and supplied by the GEC. The first 1,500-volt equipment in this country since this voltage was adopted as standard by the Ministry of Transport.'

Below: The line is still in constant use today, and is the recipient of recent investment.

Altrincham Hippodrome, Stamford Street, c. 1920

Altrincham Hippodrome (above, top left) was a large cinema theatre that opened in 1912 to a design by the architects Butterworth & Duncan. Its owners were T. Hargreaves Ltd of Altrincham. Italianate in style, it had a capacity of 1,800 in 1912. The interior was two-tier, with a large proscenium stage 27 feet wide. Live shows continued into at least the 1950s. It was later subdivided for use as a bingo hall and by the 1970s was known as the Altrincham Entertainment Centre. It was demolished in 1987 and made into offices – on the right of the modern image.

North West Road Car Company Ltd, bus nos 194 and 773, looking towards Altrincham
Based in Stockport, the North West Road Car Company Ltd had a garage on Oakfield Street, Altrincham. The company was formed in 1923, expanding their services in Northwich and Flixton through the Mid Cheshire Motor Bus Company Ltd in 1924, later becoming part of the National Bus Company. Business success continued as they acquired other companies and expanded, eventually being renamed National Travel (North West) Ltd in 1974. The company operated bus services in five counties – Cheshire, Lancashire, West Riding of Yorkshire, Derbyshire and Staffordshire. The modern image is from Oakfield Street, looking towards its junction with Oakfield Road.

Altrincham Garrick Playhouse, Barrington Road, Altrincham, c. 1940

Altrincham Garrick Society was formed in November 1913 by Walter S. Nixon and A. P. Hill. Jack Byrom offered the basement of his Kingsway drapery store as headquarters and the Little Cellar-Theatre was established. Encouraged by George Bernard Shaw, the Garrick Playhouse was eventually built. Jack Byrom cut the first sod. It was designed by T. Harold Hill, built by Charles Pennington of Hale, and opened by P. M. Oliver on 1 October 1932. The first play performed was *The Immortal Lady* by Clifford Bax. The inset image shows a programme from 1946.

View from Oldfield Brow in 1904 and Cottages on Oldfield Road, Altrincham

Oldfield Brow lies on the outskirts of Altrincham, between Oldfield Road and the Bridgewater Canal. The cottages on Oldfield Road sit at the top of the rise. Heading east, Oldfield Road joins the A56 at the convergence of Manchester Road and Church Street, with John Leigh Park on its southern corner. The 14-acre park overlooks Broadheath and was originally the grounds of Oldfield Hall, which was demolished in 1916. John Leigh of Beech Lawn, Altrincham, purchased the land and presented it to the council in 1917.

Broadheath Railway Station, *c.* 1900
Broadheath served the northern part of Altrincham and opened on 1 November 1853, closing on 10 September 1962 for passengers and completely closing on 28 December 1964. It was built by the Warrington & Altrincham Junction Railway and was renamed the Warrington & Stockport Railway shortly before the station opened. Situated on an embankment, west of the A56, it is now beneath George Richards Way, which runs in front of Halfords, behind the Railway public house. A new retail park and industrial estate are also located here. The station opened as Altrincham W & S and changed its name to Broadheath (Altrincham), in November 1856.

Navigation Road Railway Station, Altrincham, c. 1970
The station is located to the east of Altrincham. There is a level crossing at the southern end of Navigation Road and formerly a signal box, which was here from 1882 until 7 July 1991. The original railway station was opened by the Manchester, South Junction & Altrincham Railway on 20 July 1931, following electrification. The former Altrincham platform is used for Mid-Cheshire Line trains and the former Manchester platform became a Metrolink stop on 15 June 1992. Freight trains also operate through the station.

Cresta Court Hotel, Church Street, Altrincham, c. 1970

The Cresta Court Hotel is a typical mid-twentieth-century structure. It was built in a part of Altrincham that has proximity to the A56 in order to benefit from passing trade between Manchester and Chester. It is close to Manchester Airport and beneficial for tourists awaiting flights to international destinations, or visiting Altrincham town centre. Today the building has had a revamp, but its original structure is still recognisable some forty years later.

St George's Parish Church, Church Street, Altrincham, c. 1900

St George's is the parish church of Altrincham. It is a Grade II-listed building. The original church was a chapel of ease to St Mary's Church in Bowdon, and was built in 1799. The tower and spire date from 1874 and the chancel from 1886. In 1896–97, Lancaster architects Austin and Paley rebuilt the nave and aisles, with the tower remaining from the earlier church. The three lower stages of the tower are the oldest part of the church, dating from around 1829.

Interior of St George's Parish Church, Church Street, Altrincham, 1907
The church contains stained-glass windows, designed by Mary Lowndes, that date from 1895 and are located in the chancel. The first female glazier in the Arts and Crafts movement, Mary Lowndes was also an influential figure in the Suffragette organisation and designed many of their banners. St George became a separate parish in 1868. The Revd Oswald Leicester, its first curate-in-charge (1799–1831), was influential in the founding of the church. There is a memorial to him in the chancel.

St Margaret's War Memorial and St Margaret's Road, 1960

St Margaret's war memorial, in the form of a Celtic cross, honours Altrincham's fallen from both world wars. It was constructed of Portland stone and is Grade II listed, costing £1-500, by the designer George Faulkner Armitage. The unveiling ceremony took place on 13 November 1920, with the war memorial dedicated by the Bishop of Chester on the same day. The ceremony was attended by relatives and friends of the fallen. Land for the memorial garden was donated by the Earl of Stamford in 1948.

St Margaret's Parish Church, Dunham Road, Altrincham, 1916

On 11 April 1855, St Margaret's became the district church for parts of the townships of Dunham Massey and Altrincham, which were previously served by St Mary's, Bowden. It later included the chapel of Dunham Massey at All Saints. On 5 November 1867, St Margaret's boundaries were reduced when part of the township of Dunham Massey was transferred to the new district of Altrincham, St John the Evangelist. Today the church includes such activities as a Sunday school, organised children's worship and a youth group.

St Margaret's Parish Church, Dunham Road, Altrincham, c. 1930
St Margaret's was constructed between 1853 and 1855 by William Hayley and is a Grade II-listed building. It was extended westward in 1923–25 by W. Tapper, with part of this scheme remaining incomplete. The two-stage central tower had a steeple until 1927. It is a typical example of the Gothic Revival period, which preceded High Victorian Gothic. The church has a very elaborate canted Gothic panelled ceiling and tall crossing arches. There are carved screens, an organ chamber, pulpit and a selection of stained-glass windows.

Entrance to Dunham Park, Dunham Road, Altrincham, 1903
This view looks towards the now-removed spire of St Margaret's Church on Dunham Road, heading into Altrincham. The gate is now part of the public footpath leading to Dunham Forest Golf and Country Club. Bradgate Road runs to the left, forming a junction with Dunham Road, and Highgate Road forms another junction with Dunham Road, again on the left and closer to Altrincham. Today this is a very busy route for traffic into Altrincham due to access to the motorway and routes into Cheshire.

Dunham Hill, Chester Road, Bowdon, 1914
To the left of this view are the grounds of Parklands, a large Victorian mansion belonging to William Berry, whose boot polish company was involved in the launch of Cherry Blossom Boot Polish in 1906. In 1913 William Berry Ltd were bought out, but they continued to be influential in the area, building commercial developments on Stamford New Road and in Hale. The Berry family continued to live at Parklands until 1963, when the house contents were auctioned off and the property sold.

Shepherd's Cottages, Dunham Hill, Bowdon, c. 1900
This view shows the junction of Charcoal Road and Dunham Road, where there are now traffic lights at these busy crossroads. Located here (to the left) is Parklands, a fine Victorian mansion of red brick and stone. Built in 1887–88 by William Berry, it remained in the family until its sale in 1963. Until 1994 it was the base of the Institute for the Study of Hierological Values. It is now a private residence.

Lodge and Entrance to Dunham Park, 1908
The lodge and entrance to Dunham Park is located at the junction of Charcoal Road and Main Drive. This view looks from Main Drive towards Charcoal Road, heading into Altrincham on the right. Behind the photographer, Main Drive stretches through woodland of the National Trust owned Dunham Park, towards Dunham Hall. Coach and horse teams of the Earls of Stamford would have used this gateway on their way to and from church and official functions.

Dunham Town, Dunham Massey, c. 1900
Dunham Park, lying to the south of the village, was designated a Site of Special Scientific Interest in 1965 because of its biodiversity, and has been managed by the National Trust since 1976. In the Domesday Book Dunham Massey was known as 'Doneham' and belonged to the de Massey family and later the Earls of Stamford. Once part of the parish of Bowdon, the Church of St Mark's, built in 1856, stands at the junction of Back Lane and School Lane.

Dunham Massey Railway Station, Henshall Lane, 1962

Opening in June 1854, Dunham Massey station closed on 10 September 1962. It was on the Warrington Arpley to Skelton Junction line, which opened in 1852–53. Now a private dwelling, the station was on the south side of Henshall Lane and was named Warburton from its opening until June 1856, when it became Warburton and Dunham. In October 1856 it was renamed Dunham, finally becoming Dunham Massey in April 1861, until 1962. Freight trains used the line until 7 July 1985.

Bowdon Park, 1906
At the road bend where Dunham Road joins Highgate Road and Bradgate Road there is a wooden gate and stile (one of many throughout the park), which leads into the woodland at Dunham New Park. This path tracks through some beautiful oak woodland and becomes a wider path. This area is now taken over mainly by the golf course, but was once used as an American army base and then as a German prisoner of war camp during the Second World War.

Beech Avenue, Dunham Park, 1953
The original site of Dunham Hall was a moated location. The hall stood empty for around fifty years at the end of the nineteenth century, until the 9th Earl moved to Dunham in June 1906. The 10th Earl, Roger Grey, remained unmarried and arranged before his death for the property to go to the National Trust as his nephew did not want it. He died on 18 August 1976 and the hall and gardens opened to the public in April 1981.

Dunham Park, 1955

Dunham Massey's deer park covers 192.7 acres, featuring formal avenues and wood pasture and parkland. It is home to an impressive collection of ancient trees, some dating from the seventeenth century. Owned by the National Trust, it is considered a site of national importance. In 1917 Penelope, Lady Stamford, transformed Dunham Massey Hall into an auxiliary hospital; 281 patients passed through Stamford Military Hospital in almost two years.

Dunham Park fallow deer, 1952
Dunham Massey's deer park is occupied by a herd of fallow deer that have been resident at Dunham for hundreds of years. The fallow deer in the park are very tame and tolerant of visitors.

The Hall, Dunham Park, 1910
There was once a Norman castle on the site and a chapel was known to have existed as early as 1307. Sir George Booth (1566–1652) built a house around a courtyard in the early seventeenth century, although little of this now remains. The main house was remodelled by John Norris between 1732 and 1740 in the time of George, 2nd Earl of Warrington, with minor additions by John Shaw in 1822. Further alterations were made by Joseph Compton Hall in the Edwardian period.

Reception of the Earl of Stamford, Dunham Hall, 8 August 1906

This photograph was taken on the lawns in front of Dunham Hall at the reception to mark the Earl of Stamford's return to Dunham. Shown are Lady Jane Grey (Later Lady Jane Turnbull), the Countess of Stamford, the Earl of Stamford, and Roger Grey – the 10th and final Earl of Stamford – whose life's work is now preserved by the National Trust. Some well-known local dignitaries at the reception included Mr. A. Marshal Higham and Mr Tom Johnson, headmaster of Seamons Moss School.

Old Mill, Dunham Park, Bowdon, c. 1905

The saw mill (originally a corn mill) was Grade II listed on 12 July 1985, and was probably built in 1616 (definitely pre-1697) in the time of 'old' Sir George Booth. It is a rare working example of a seventeenth-century watermill, which was restored, with machinery reconstructed, in around 1980. On the ground floor is the reconstructed, overshot waterwheel and a lathe. On the first floor is the carpenter's shop, frame saw, wood boring machine and circular saw. The attic was formerly a granary.

Groby Road, Altrincham, c. 1950

This is named after the village of Groby in Leicestershire, the birthplace of Lady Jane Grey. The Church of St Vincent de Paul (see inset) was opened at the junction of Groby Road and Bentinck Road on 1 October 1905, replacing the chapel in New Street. The cost was estimated to be approximately £6,000, with the first sod being cut on 29 October 1903. Designed by Edmund Kirby of Liverpool, the church seated 500 and was constructed in the Early English Gothic style. It was opened by Dr Allen, Bishop of Shrewsbury.

The Downs, Altrincham, 1907
The growth of Bowdon as a residential area began in the 1840s, with landowners selling parcels of farmland to developers and the opening of Bowdon railway station in 1849 to commuters. The clean air and tranquillity of the Bowdon Downs was attractive to both developers and potential residents. The first properties to be constructed were terraced and semi-detached houses, but by the 1860s and 1870s merchants began to build larger villas on Green Walk. They remain a feature today.

St John the Evangelist, junction of Ashley Road and St John's Road, Altrincham, c. 1910

St John the Evangelist was built in 1866 as a chapel to Altrincham, St George. In 1867 it became the district church for parts of the townships of Altrincham, Dunham Massey and Hale, which were previously served by Dunham Massey, St Margaret's; Timperley, Christ Church; and St Mary's. There were further boundary changes on 31 July 1906 when part of the township of Hale was transferred to St Peter's, thus reducing St John's parish boundary area as a result.

Delamer and St John's Cross Roads, Altrincham, 1959
These leafy suburban roads are in Altrincham. Observe above the original gas lamps and authentic 1950s motor transport parked close to the road junction. Delamer (not Delamere) Road is named after George Booth, the 1st Lord Delamer. In 1684 the town bell was given to Altrincham by the 2nd Lord Delamer and installed in the bell tower above the clock in the old town hall – next to the Unicorn Hotel and now the Old Market Tavern – where the bell was located on the staircase.

The Firs, Altrincham, 1911
The Firs was developed in the mid-nineteenth century and forms a junction at the village of Bowdon with Stamford Road, Green Walk and Church Brow at its centre and directly opposite Bowdon's parish church. From here the road heads in a northerly direction towards Altrincham, joining St Margaret's Road, which heads towards Dunham Road and Cavendish Road, then towards Ashley Road in the east. The photograph below shows another leafy suburban scene, where there is a modern synagogue (see inset).

Altrincham Grammar School for Girls, junction of Cavendish Road and Bowdon Road, c. 1975

The biggest girls' grammar school in England was officially opened on Monday, 4 July 1910 by His Honour Judge J. K. Bradbury MA, Chairman of the Board of Governors, and witnessed by the first headmistress, Miss Howes Smith MA, and local dignitaries. On 14 September 1910 the school opened to sixty boys and girls, with eight members of staff. Sports were played on the back lawn (visible above). In 1974 the school changed its name from Altrincham County High School to Altrincham Grammar School for Girls. Shown in the modern image is the grammar school's entrance at the junction of Cavendish Road and Bowdon Road.

Langham Road, Bowdon, 1908
The cottages on the right date from 1640; in 1908 they were still thatched and ivy-clad. The wall opposite, surrounding Bowdon parish church's graveyard, is a Grade II-listed structure. Located on the south side of Langham Road is the Grade II-listed Bowdon Old Hall, dated around 1700, with later nineteenth-century additions. Recently around 150 lots from Bowdon Old Hall came up for auction. These included a collection of antique furniture, pictures and ceramics from the home of Lord John Lee of Trafford.

Bowdon village and parish church, c. 1900
The Griffin public house is shown on the right of the photograph above, opposite Bowdon parish church. There are four distinct areas – Dunham Massey, Warburton, Bowdon and Bowdon Vale. Bowdon is the largest ward in the Metropolitan Borough of Trafford, which was formed in 1974. Before this it was historically a part of Cheshire. From 1894 Bowdon was known as Bowdon Urban District. Prior to this it was Bowdon Local Board in 1864, and then Bowdon Urban Sanitary District from 1875–94.

The Church of St Mary the Virgin, Stamford Road, Bowden, c. 1900
There has been a church at this location since Saxon times, when a small community was established in the seventh century by Archbishop Theodore. Bowdon is mentioned in the Domesday Book (1086) as having a mill, church and parish priest at 'Bogedone' (which means bow-shaped hill), held by the Norman Hamon de Massey. In around 1100 the church was rebuilt in stone, with a tower and other alterations were added c. 1320. It was partially rebuilt in 1510, but not completed.

St Mary's Churchyard, Stamford Road, Bowdon, 1905

In the churchyard there are three Grade II-listed structures. The first is a sandstone sundial post of unknown date. There is also a sandstone war memorial from around 1920, by Arthur Hennings. The third structure is the piers, railings and walls surrounding the churchyard.

Church Brow Cottages, Church Brow, Bowdon, 1904
The cottage to the right was occupied by a Miss Lightfoot, joint owner with her sister of nearby Lightfoot's Tea Garden. The second cottage was originally one house and was once occupied by Mr Sutton, caretaker at Bowdon Assembly Rooms. Below him lived John Hassall, of Alderley's Farm, Bowdon. In the fifth cottage lived Ann and John Taylor, a teams-man at Alderley's Farm. The cottage below the passage was thatched up to 1914. The Grade II-listed Bowdon Old Forge is located here.

South Downs Road, Bowdon, 1904
Known as Ashley Heath, this area of South Downs Road now has a tall hedge running along the right-hand side of the road, where there is still a postbox today. The junction here was wider in 1904 and there is an earth bank and hedges directly opposite, which was removed and replaced by a stone wall with a wooden fence by 1906. Today the stone walls remain, but with taller hedges and additional iron fencing.

Ashley Heath, Bowdon, 1906
In the late nineteenth century many of the residents of Bowdon were business owners, building large villas and mansion houses in what was still a semi-rural area. This is reflected by the fact that mains water appeared in 1864 and gas lighting by 1865. The district's agricultural past was honoured by the annual Altrincham Show, which was held on the Devisdale in Bowdon until 1966. Farmers attended the show from all over the country in order to exhibit cattle.

Off South Downs Road, Bowdon, *c.* 1900 and present-day luxury properties, 2016

South Downs Road is also home to Bowdon Cricket Club (see inset), which was founded in 1856, renting the ground from the 7th Earl of Stamford. The grounds pavilion was constructed in 1874 and still has its original façade. In 1939 Helen Bickham bought the ground from the 10th Earl of Stamford in memory of her brother, Ernest Bickham, and then donated it to the cricket club. Cheshire have played here on a number of occasions from 1910–2001.

Castle Mills and Weir, Castle Mill Lane, 1909 and summertime at Ashley Mill, *c*. 1910
The River Bollin runs to the south of Altrincham and provided Edwardian children with a source of amusement on sunny summer days, as shown in the Ashley Mill photo below. Where Castle Mill Lane crosses the River Bollin, at Castle Mills and Weir near Ringway, there was an outdoor swimming pool with a disinfectant foot bath before bathers could enter the water. The pool was cold, dirty and crowded. It was filled in around the 1970s and a Spanish-style villa was then constructed in the grounds.

Hale Railway Station, Ashley Road, 1906

Hale station is 8 miles south-west of Manchester Piccadilly and was originally named Bowdon Peel Causeway by the Cheshire Midland Railway. It opened on 12 May 1862, initially running from Altrincham to Knutsford. The Cheshire Midland Railway was finally amalgamated into the Cheshire Lines Committee on 15 August 1867, with the company remaining independent until the establishment of British Rail in 1948. Bowdon Peel Causeway became Peel Causeway on 1 January 1899, and on the same date in 1902 it was renamed Hale.

Hale Railway Station, Ashley Road, 1911

This view of the centre of Hale in 1911 shows the railway station on the right-hand side and the signal box next to it. The level crossing allows traffic to cross Ashley Road, where a cyclist can be seen on a somewhat wet day. Today there are modern residential developments opposite the signal box. On the far left is the Cheshire Midland public house, named after the company who constructed the Altrincham–Knutsford section of the line and station, which opened on 12 May 1862.

RAILWAY STATION, HALE.
PERFECTION SERIES 1268.

Hale Railway Station and Signal Box, Ashley Road, *c.* 1900
The station is Grade II listed and the listed signal box of 1876 closed on 22 July 1991. The goods yard closed on 2 December 1963. The arrival of the railway in the mid-nineteenth century saw the village of Hale change from having an agricultural base, to becoming a commuter area for the middle classes and merchants serving the city of Manchester. Next to the station is the Cheshire Midland public house, which has a very distinctive pub sign showing the company's coat of arms.

The last Pull & Push, Hale, 12 February, 1966

This was the original Pull & Push Farewell Railtour, organised by the Locomotive Club of Great Britain. Due to demand there was a duplicate tour, which ran on Saturday 5 February 1966. Both used the locomotive No. 41286. The route ran from Earlestown to Warrington Bank Quay, Hartford Junction (LNW and CLC), Middlewich, Sandbach, Hale, Skelton Junction, Warrington (Arpley), Ditton Junction, Farnworth and Bold, St Helens (Shaw St), St Helens Junction, returning to Earlestown. Below: Another view of the station today.

Ashley Road, Hale, 1907

This was once known as Thorley Moor Lane at Altrincham. Sometime before 1912, the road had been widened from a rough track thanks to the financial generosity of Mr J. H. Brown, who purchased all the land necessary for the improvements. This included farmland to the west of Willowtree Road, up to Ashley Road. He also built the terraced houses on the lower side of Willowtree Road and constructed station buildings in Altrincham. The Wilson Rest Gardens were at the junction with Hale Road.

St Peter's Church, Ashley Road, Hale, 1934

The church was dedicated on 16 June 1892. It was originally a chapel to St Mary's Church (Bowden) and from 1906 a district church for part of the township of Hale. It was previously served by St Mary's (Bowden), and St John the Evangelist. From 2007 to 26 January 2015 Libby Lane was vicar of the combined benefice of St Peter's in Hale and St Elizabeth's in Ashley. She was the first female to be appointed as a bishop by the Church of England.

Park Road, Hale, 1963
Park Road stretches from its junction with Ashley Road in the west, to its junction with Hale Road at its eastern end. It is one of the wide, leafy roads that are typical of the area. Note also the sandstone walls, which are widespread in this district and make use of the stone once quarried here. The photograph dates from the days when the volume of traffic was not as great as today and parking was much less of an issue!

Bankhall Lane and Wyngate Road Junction, Hale, c. 1930
This photograph looks towards Ashley Road and the railway bridge, which crosses the Chester to Manchester railway line. Many of the properties in this area are Edwardian in design and still overlook fields, having changed little in the intervening years. Bankhall Lane is also close to the River Bollin and its picturesque countryside walks. It is within easy walking distance of the village of Hale. Set in a tranquil suburban location, it is also near to Altrincham town centre.

Mission Church, *c.* 1905 and Hale Chapel Sunday School, 2016, Hale Road, Hale Barns, Altrincham

The Mission Church was built 1881, opening on St Paul's Day 1882 and adopting this name. It was a chapel to Ringway St Mary and All Saints, closing 1967, with Hale Barns All Saints built on the site. The Unitarian chapel on Chapel Lane was built in 1723 for the Presbyterians. The congregation pioneered education in the district, building a day school in 1740 on Hale Road. The school building is from around 1880 and the schoolmaster's house from the mid-eighteenth century. The village is named after the now demolished Tithe Barns.

Stockport Road, 1904 and the Stonemasons Arms (inset), Timperley Village, 2016

The name Timperley can be traced back to 1070. The spelling has changed several times but the name means 'a stone outcrop in a woodland clearing'. Sited on solid sandstone, the area was widely used for stone quarrying, although the quarries are now disused. Large blocks of sandstone were known as 'tymps.' Evidence of this stone quarrying can still be seen today in the shape of gateposts and stone walls bordering gardens, particularly along the main roads, including Stockport Road, shown above.

Woodlands Hotel, Timperley, c. 1950

The hotel shares its name with the Woodlands Park estate in Timperley, which was described as 'Manchester's sunniest suburb' and 'the ideal residential district'. It is located on Woodlands Road/Stockport Road, opposite Altrincham golf course. In the late 1850s Manchester entrepreneur Samuel Brooks bought several hundred acres of farmland in Timperley, with the intention of developing it for housing. A new estate of large houses at Woodlands Park was built and continued to develop until the late 1920s to early 1930s.

Heyesleigh Auxiliary Military Hospital, Heyes Lane, Timperley, 1918
This postcard photograph is of Heyesleigh, the auxiliary military hospital at Heyes Lane, Timperley. The handwritten reverse of the card begins, 'Timperley 25.04.18. Dearest Mum, Dad thought you would like to have a photograph of our Red Cross. Quite a nice place isn't it?' It was originally the home of Dr Louis Savatard and became a hospital in 1914, with Pickering Lodge annexed to it in 1915. This brought the total number of beds available to ninety-eight.

Park Road, Timperley, c. 1930

Park Road is shown near the railway station (to the right above), and the MSJ&AR line between Manchester and Altrincham. The Stockport, Timperley and Altrincham Junction was opened in 1866, leading to the demolition of several cottages on Park Road and the crossing of three roads – Stockport Road, Park Road and Moss Lane – as well as the canal. The MSJ&AR lines crossed near Deansgate Lane, which is around half a mile from here, heading towards Altrincham. Known as Skelton Junction, traffic included freight trains serving the chemical works near Northwich. Inset: Frank Sidebottom's statue, Timperley Village, 2016.

Timperley Railway Station, Park Road, c. 1950
To the south of Timperley station was Timperley Junction signal box, which was constructed in 1897. It contained forty levers and was decommissioned on 10 October 1965. In more recent times Metrolink provided a central reversal siding, just to the south of the station. The station and lines occupy a narrow strip of land between the Bridgewater Canal (to the west) and residential properties (to the east). The bridge, carrying Park Road and providing access to the station, spans both the canal and Metrolink.

Timperley Railway Station, Park Road, c. 1910
Timperley station was opened on 20 July 1849 by the MSJ&AR and closed to electric trains, as did all the stations on this section of line, on 24 December 1991. This was to allow the construction of the Metrolink tram system, which terminates at Altrincham. The canopy on the Manchester-bound platform was demolished in August 2009 and the former booking office was used by a taxi firm for many years, until 2003. In spring 2010 it became a coffee shop.

Timperley Railway Station, First Electric Train, 1931
Shown is an electric train to Altrincham on the first day of service in 1931. A contemporary noted:

> Many people will wonder why the new trains are built on the compartment style instead of the saloon type, which has been the custom recently. It appears at first to be a retrograde idea, but when it is realised that the train only stops at a station for fifteen seconds, passengers can be discharged and taken up much more rapidly by the compartment system than by any other.

Westwood Avenue, Timperley, c. 1930
Timperley's residential property was once agricultural land well into the eighteenth century and market gardening well into the nineteenth, in order to provide for the rapidly expanding city of Manchester. In earlier times, the medieval site of Timperley Old Hall was close to the present day Timperley Hall, which became a pub restaurant, at Altrincham golf course. The moated manor house of Timperley Old Hall has been subject to extensive archaeological excavations and dates to 1560, replacing an earlier structure.

St John the Baptist Roman Catholic Church, Thorley Lane, Timperley, c. 1960
The parish began in 1957, separating from St Hugh's parish, with the acquisition of a large house on Thorley Lane. Father Joseph Taggart was appointed parish priest. Three years later the new parish had its own church, designed by Francis Reynolds in traditional style – long and narrow – with a separate baptistery. The Church of St John the Baptist closed after Mass on Trinity Sunday (7 June) 2009. It was demolished in April 2013 and the site was sold for retirement homes.

Mayfield Road, Timperley, c. 1960
Mayfield Road forms a junction with Stockport Road in the centre of Timperley village. Its junction is opposite Timperley Methodist Church (see inset) which has been at this site since 1937. Mayfield Road is another typical leafy suburban road, developed when much of Timperley and the surrounding area was given over to housing in the 1930s. Shown in the photograph from around 1960 are semi-detached houses of typical 1930s style.

Also available from Amberley Publishing

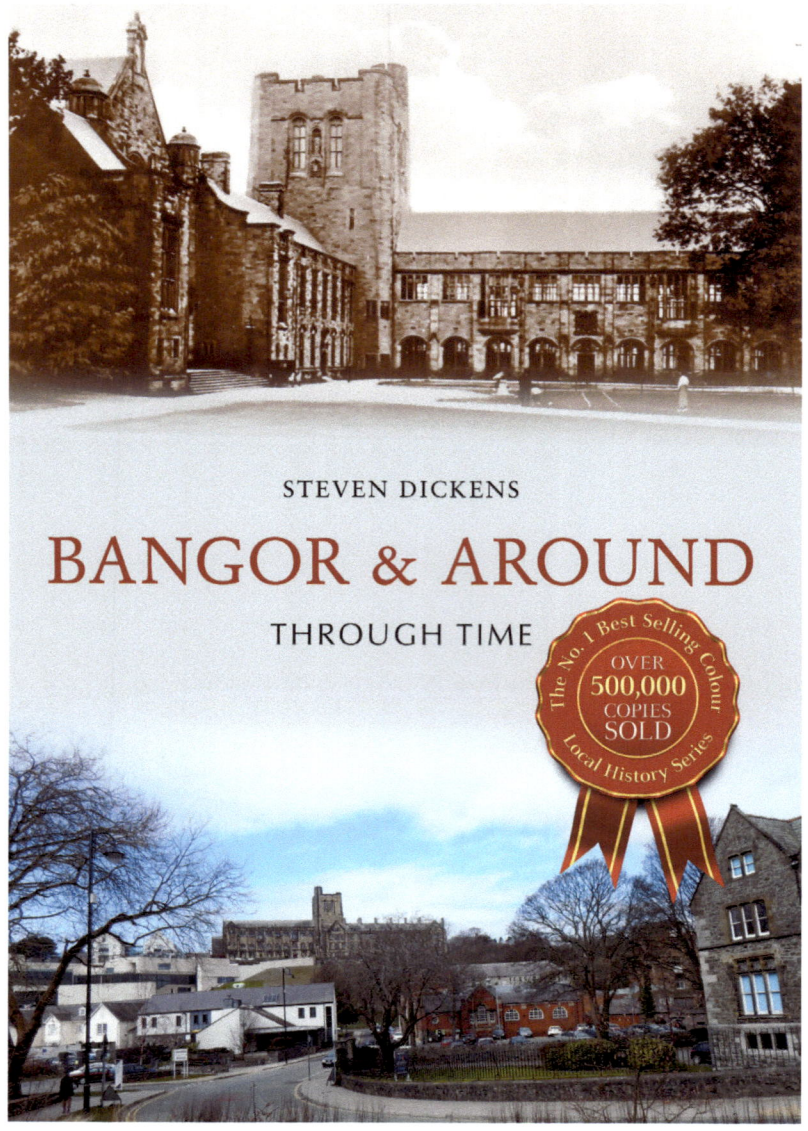

This fascinating selection of photographs traces some of the many ways in which Bangor & Around has changed and developed over the last century.
978 1 4456 3278 0
Available to order direct 01453 847 800
www.amberley-books.com